Toy Park

Toy Park

Poems by Beau Boudreaux

Cherry Grove Collections

Published by Cherry Grove Collections

P.O. Box 541106

Cincinnati, OH 45254-1106

ISBN: 9781625493248

Poetry Editor: Kevin Walzer

Business Editor: Lori Jareo

Visit us on the web at www.cherry-grove.com

Acknowledgments

Grateful acknowledgment is made to the editors of the following publications, where these poems, some in earlier versions, originally appeared.

Agave Press: "Saturday," "Wedding Ring"
Aji Magazine: "Discipline"
Foliate Oak Literary Magazine: "Close Cal"
Gravel: "What's Left"
Linden Avenue Literary Journal: "Disclosure," "First Trimester"
Louisiana Literature: "Boulevard," End of July"
Mojave River Review: "Married"
Naugatuck River Review: "Big Boy"
Noctua Journal: "Dr. D."
Orange Quarterly: "Domesticity," "Recurrent Dream"
The Paddlewheeler: "Medusa"
Panoplyzine: "Polynesia," "Toy Park"
Sediments Literary Arts Journal: "Destin"
Sheepshead Review: "Crib," "Southern California"
Switchback: "Rhys' Shoe"
Thirty West Publishing House: "Decadence"
Torrid Literature Journal: "Worry Bone"
The Winnow Magazine: "Toby"

For Rhys

Contents

II.

III.

IV.

I.

Avant-Garde Love

Why go out for hamburger
when I can have steak at home?
Paul Newman

Southern woman with emerald eyes
I courted she drove six hours round trip

every other weekend in her old Honda
sold her home in Madison, moved in

down in New Orleans
her black lab with my ageing beagle…

six years, I've looked forward
each peerless moment, even mundane—

her blonde wisps on bed sheets
crease in her thigh after a jog

surprise Chardonnay chilled
after work, crock pot on Sunday—

when I sour when I'm wrong…
her stolid voice cool demeanor

why I come straight home from the gym
along St. Charles as girls in tank tops jog by.

Married

A catcher's mitt
worn leather snug on the hand

palm toughened by countless evenings
our fastballs and curves—

dinners where we dress out our china
as the home team, smug heads of the table

long days of extra innings
take their swings, garbage at the curb

pitch and catch from the mound
keep an eye on her signals

wordless nod
chance to steal or get picked off

under blue horizons, occasional sunsets
our crowd chanting in the stands.

First Trimester

In the afternoon
my wife tires

during the night
has to pee four or five times—

the ultrasound my awakening
as the technician slips me the image,

late April one morning sick
carries on throughout the day

sleeping through the night…
my only wish her recovery

the next day she pivots
a new moat surrounds her fort.

May

First true signs of a paunch
her black slacks for work won't button

there's salvation at the maternity store
smart dresses and skirts

May is fleeting, we're almost half-way
like rookie training camp, ahead

house renovations, the yellow hue
from Ace Hardware

for the room, crib
still in the box, stern reminders

what I never noticed to proof—
electrical sockets, vents

she says our entire house
could use better cleaning

the scorching summer, hurricane
prepared like uncrossing fingers.

Domesticity

Sag in the driver's seat, sigh
idling for the green streetcar while

tourists unload in July heat
look both ways crossing the neutral ground

over tracks to reach safely across
the avenue—I barely accelerate

air conditioner cool on low
they're building a new house

on my block, progress in the morning
before afternoon thunderstorms roll in—

plan creole tomatoes, sweet corn, watermelon
perhaps boiled gulf shrimp on a bed of lettuce,

more dire tasks, strange leak
from the bathroom ceiling

during heavy showers, toddler's loose
front tooth, rattle in the dryer—

my wife returns soon from work
like aloe on my sun-burned skin

her blonde hair freshly clipped
at the shoulder, black dress

she slips into comfortable clothes
white t-shirt, jeans, espadrilles

I turn on the local jazz station.
put her Chardonnay on ice.

Hump Day

Jameson helps wind the day down
like a rubber stop releases an open door...

wake to the baby boy crying in his crib,
change diaper, wife at yoga

read the *New York Times,* the *Advocate*
respond to emails, check Fed Ex deliveries

my wife comes home
I leave and meet Joan to sign off

papers for my house
I lived in for a decade

get gas, at Shell
pick up prescriptions, razors at CVS

return to take the boy to the backyard
and talk to David in Los Angeles

while my wife goes for her flu shot
check the stock market close

change and rush to the gym for an hour,
return home, work on poetry, she

feeds the boy, nurtures his bath, says night-night
to the humidified vault of his crib...

a glass of Pinot Grigio for my wife
for me a little ice to finish the day.

Sons and Daughters

People ask *you going to have another one?*
Recall my wife across the table

our first date night saying she was so happy with one
willing for a second try while I wide-eyed,

enjoying the cocktail let that slide by, even the cleaners
ask when a brother or sister is coming

on a Saturday afternoon my wife inquires
don't you want a sibling for your son?

Infant clothes packed and toys given away
extra bedroom now a guest room

in less than nine months our family blossoms
son grew to toddler, wine stocks in the cellar

we play tennis again, summer washes over us
in waves of heat, home offices upgraded,

trip to the Gulf coast, a staycation downtown—
I think often, fear for a little one, our risks,

my trepidation to cross
back over the baby bridge

our urge to have children before forty
a balloon that slowly loses air.

Obsession

Suddenly, I've stoked
a crazy love affection

for my wife, as if she's on film,
sway away or towards me

groove in her thigh as she fills
a glass of cool water

her petite body, healthy foods—
kale salad, kiwi, dark chocolate,

did I mention the Barre class three times a week
and those legs that late summer tan,

as she dries a dish, net of lemons
her blonde hair my waterfall

when we met—and think
she carried our child just

a year ago, mint scent when
she slides under our covers.

Wet Lips

Fresh cut yellow tulips don't last long
wilt in the vase, canaries gasping for air—

before the reading a close friend
tells me another couple divorced

leaves a lasting bruise on my night
as I drive by their house for sale…

I think about making love to my wife
in the early afternoon while my toddler

takes his deep nap, having her
just return from work in a crème suit

her perfume lingers
like jasmine crowding the vine,

still sweet this April
as amber honey, my spoon scoops from the jar.

Distance

Takes around three hours
no matter how fast I drive

learned not to bring roses
they wilt backseat

but found a Kroger a few blocks
from her house on Magnolia Street

florist recognizes me from habit
two tries to write her a heartfelt card

ten times out of ten she's home
seen through the window

alone just returned from work
slowly twisting her blond hair

house stocked with wine
pillows, candles...

afterwards, we toast
a chilled bottle of champagne

weekends of tangled sheets
gently floating to sleep, anchored boats

and walks through woods—if not for work
I wouldn't go back to New Orleans.

Jalousie

I cannot change her past
slip ups, ex lovers in L.A.

our long chatty car rides
remarks about sexy actors

so I try to shut the blind
stop being a witness in conversation—

candid images—tipsy
talk over cocktails

on our fifth date—I remember
what she said better than my own

discreet memories, her specifics hung
like low bearing fruit brushed my chest

as she came back from the bathroom
catching eyes in a navy dress

all the way back to my table
men hitting on her.

Solar Plexus

Another long day chopping wood
mixing a cocktail

wisp of blonde behind her ear
I'm demanding, not rolling

with today's punch
and she will stand for another

round tomorrow to dance around
verbal jabs take

this toll, I gambol, plea
a ring should not be square.

Vacation Again

This dawns the first morning
in the pool with my toddler and wife

stubble on my chin—could I've neglected
to bring my razor on vacation again?

I joked not to forget our son much less sunscreen,
close my eyes underwater

picture my leather dopp kit
with travel size shave cream, trial size toothpaste

and sample toothbrush from the dentist,
a ten percent chance I've packed everything

when we return to the room and check—
left my razor on the bathroom counter at home.

For most, not a big deal, over years
I forced myself to purchase razors

now I turn to my wife's toiletries
oh, this looks promising—pink, three blades

white tea scented gel bars for glide
and ask if she minds if I shave with her Gillette Venus?

I lather up, hold the soft sleek handle
and begin my routine—Venus when wet

forms its own foam. I make little progress
can't not stroke against the grain,

what normally takes two minutes
takes five. In the shower I feel spots Venus missed

so I go back over...this razor is not cut for the face
but can pinch hit for a few days—my wife says Venus

is a wonder on her legs in a hot bath.

Hostess

Our cocktail party, glimpse
across the room my wife converses

like owning a Degas
someone would die to steal—

lightning strike as she turns my way
her emerald eyes, voice of chimes

she works the room, chatting
about children, work, movies

far better host
than I with a half full wine glass

tipsy on the couch pillows
talking Saints playoff hopes

year after year
my one jardinière.

Polynesia

The god Maui opened the door
paths illumed

like diving into a cool lagoon
to witness a slow sunset

my skiff sails into harbor
a wind-kissed Saturday afternoon.

Surprise saturnalia
warm, dense sand,

in the surf counting waves
till I reach the highest

opening another Chardonnay
listening to my wife sing

my favorite chanteuse
through the swell

gently rocks then dreams
carry me off

like a letter sealed in a bottle
bobbing out to sea.

Wedding Ring

Missing when I put my hand
on the steering wheel—first time not on my finger,

never slipped off in the sink
or shower, now naked tan lines—no clue

where it lies—I'd opened our new toddler car seat
wedged it from the box— check nothing in the box,

recycling bin, and grass by the curb—I'd taken Rhys
on his trike—I search the sidewalk

kick the grass along the fringe not once,
not twice but three times…

would a metal detector be too drastic?
Habit my ring never left my finger like wearing eyeglasses—

must sit a moment, recall before lunch at Danneel Park
tapping the ring on the jungle gym

Rhys slapped back in laughter
Heather comes home, I give her the news

magnifying the loss. She ransacks the car's trunk,
walks the block hunting for the silver band with fresh eyes.

By dark, I've exhausted the search, dress for work
Heather jokes about keeping the girls away in class…

the ring like earning a medal, having it stolen
I can't replace it...

grab a flashlight, speed back to the park
maybe someone put up a note

or it glistens there in the grass—
sentiment creeps in spurts, the ring blessed at our wedding
ceremony

on my hand for my child's birth, for all of the holidays and
vacations.
That is what I miss, miss most...

I feel I left the club of married men
that I had taken for granted.

II.

Boulevard

A block away, a divide all the way down
Napoleon lies smooth with cut grass,
the same distance from either curb

antique lights illume
the avenue, Broadmoor
now carves a bike path...

when I used to box
sought shelter in the neutral corner
looking left and right

at the Saint's game Sunday, a linebacker
was flagged in the neutral zone
for not lining up with the ball

I rarely put my car in neutral
feels temporary, unstable
I can shift either way

there're neutral colors—light gray
beige, very hip at the gym
but they need a touch of blue and yellow

during Carnival, the place to catch
a parade, beads, and doubloons
put up a ladder, or just melt back into the crowd

where do I stand on issues
start from the neutral ground
and look both ways.

Half Shell

Early October, first chill
crave raw oysters—lemons
horseradish, Tabasco...

can drive less than a mile
for P. J's shucked salty oysters
from the local grocer

walk a half block to Superior Grill
order a dozen shucked
even charbroiled

wash down my throat
like babies on a slide
wet with cold Dixie beer.

Chocolate Freeze

There's nothing equal to sate
the palette on a humid summer afternoon—

ride the streetcar up St. Charles
to the bend in the river

grab a stool at Camellia Grill—
the best diner in town

waiters in white pour cool glasses
of water and take your order on a chit

finger a crisp five dollar bill
which includes tip

pucker your lips—ice cream
over whole milk and shaved ice—

blended thick, cool
through the straw.

West End

There's a point across
from the lighthouse where teenagers
park as waves crash the seawall

couples drink cold cans of Dixie
men cast out into the lake
redfish and speckled trout

on the horizon the sky opens
for sunset bonfire—

Bucktown a kiss away
breeze through not catching lights
Schaefer Seafood on the corner

bounty straight from Pontchartrain—
soft-shell crabs, boiled crawfish
delectable in the spring

pay cash here cheaper they say
than any credit card.

Art of the Boiled Egg

Finesse and repetition
births a fine boiled egg

medium sized steel pot
lay, gently, not two

but three large brown eggs
cover an inch and a half

with cool tap water,
lid and turn

stove to high heat—
twenty seconds

cut the flames
let simmer

exactly four minutes
slowly empty the hot water

always mindful—
douse the cooked eggs

with ice-cold water
place in a porcelain bowl

inside the fridge—
a treat later, yolk a hint creamy,

hatching into the mouth
temptation to eat two more.

Trojan Horse

Not a pleasant sight on Tuesday at 2:15pm—
computer erupts, speakers blast

malicious, my files ransacked
a number to call flashing

on the screen—I'm intrigued
this slow afternoon, opt to call

the number in red on my monitor…
a foreign man tells me he's from Microsoft

my personal information, banking, credit cards
accessed by a hacker…I hear him out

recklessly lend him access to remotely
roam my computer…but an alarm

in my head goes off
I hit the power and reboot

cleanse my drivers, run malware
like finding a nail in a car tire

slowly lets out air
plug the hole like a mechanic.

Saturday

Spring 1978
I watch bass fishing shows

through the morning—first Bill Dance
from Tennessee tossed jigs in timber

reeling in respectable largemouth.
The next half hour came Jimmy Houston

donned sunglasses, suntan, and spinnerbaits
casting into private ponds in Texas—to my chagrin

he'd kiss the catch and release...
last to follow, Roland Martin,

patrolled Okeechobee, the large Florida strain
using live shiners under cork,

caught more fish than dynamite.

Vainglory

Down here in Sportsman's Paradise
you rarely hear about the one that got away

talk about the big fish
landed, on camera—iPhone—

9 pound speckled trout from Pontchartrain,
redfish over 35 in the shallows off Cocodrie—

we know, for best eating, the fish in the ice chest
barely over the legal limit

in recent years there've been stories
of releasing record fish, maybe tagging

but don't believe it—taxidermists still have business
as trophy fish mount our walls.

Old Wood Desk

Green bank lamps light up
three framed diplomas,

there's a land line blinking
in the left corner, atomic clock

with indoor and outdoor temperature,
beer stein from my mother-in-law

holds a ruler, box of paper clips, scissors
and voter I.D. cards

on the right, an HD radio plays classical
Port-of-Call cup jammed with brass-headed tacks

dusty tape dispenser
props a frayed rhyming dictionary, silver

pocket flashlight handy, yellow screwdriver,
saving a burnt out LED

coverless paperback thesaurus
begging a word

half-glass of tap water—
envelope full of stamps, a modest collection

pale blue LOVE, yellow rose, toy truck,
Legends of Jazz at 32 cents

dare I open the drawer that takes
repeated months to clear

like a cluttered garage, dusty attic.

Goldfish

I had just moved to a new
house with a white marble pond

waterfall flowing
shallow pool—

I was told goldfish would solve
the pool's mosquito problem

I headed to Petco
where Pete took me back

to a room of aquariums
one tank held hundreds of goldfish—

he scooped a baker's dozen
tied in a plastic bag

I gently placed on my passenger seat
careful not to spill

reached home
releasing the goldfish into the water

feast for my prize pets
creating a feeding frenzy.

The Gym

Would call myself
a gym rat, devout

everyday, between noon
and six I'm in that set,

slide my card into *Simply Fit*
as if I was entering an enormous

wine cellar or tidy grocery store
of weights and machines

I lift for thirty minutes—
chest on Monday, biceps

Tuesday, back, shoulders
and biceps for Friday—

my cardio on the elliptical
watching ESPN as friends

come and go,
final stretch, wave

fist bump with trainers
on my way out the door.

Worry Bone

I left Jackson on the patio

sunning himself on his back
pushing 100 degrees I forgot

the pond and could trace
his wet paw prints on the kitchen floor—

to the hose and an oatmeal bath
where he does not complain

during a scrub down
on his neck, a knot balloons

and over the course of the day
I become concerned, deliberate

if he should get checked at the vet
oh the woe of the waiting room

the verdict is in just another
lipoma on an aging beagle.

Second Tuesday

Day the garbage truck didn't come
this time I hadn't forgotten

put the bin on the curb
in awe at first—

walked down my block
to see neighbor's green bins lined

like soldiers, I'm not the only one—
is this due to sweltering heat

it's after six
sanitation office closed

as if my call
would make a difference—

hope no one's injured
accidents can happen

my ears peeled to hear
that screech and rev

roll down my street like a late
package from UPS

the things I take for granted
like water from the faucet.

Toby

Family dinner, my wife across
the table gave in, we should get a puppy,

especially for our son, a substitute
sibling—we'd discussed and let slide

off the future…I wanted a male beagle,
tri-color with enormous ears, checked the market

found one in a small town in Missouri
ready to leave his mom just before

Christmas…he'd fly cargo direct on Delta
first flight of the morning, we're anxious

trip to PetSmart in preparation, prayed
for mild weather drove out to the airport

at noon—people picking up
their pets, my surprise a yellow Chihuahua

with my name, I double-check, a mix-up
mine flew to Norfolk

worse than a sinking stomach at the carousel
wonder what he's thinking— if he's warm, fed,

perhaps the other family
might keep him—so I returned around

midnight, not a soul in cargo
my crate, my baby beagle crying his way home.

Equity

You make a lot of money
But you just want more

Mick Jagger

Middle ground—middle of the road
not too high, not too low

long term investment provides a stream
that fills the moat

deposits, electronic wires
transactions— buy the dip

as this deepens, cavernous curve
bell finally closes…

I workout at the gym
forget during that hour

walk the beagle
a few blocks—water azaleas

wind down in the vault of shower
Irish Spring, Head and Shoulders

shave and pour a Scotch
cook Blue Runner red beans and rice

Cajun sausage, family dinner
with toddler and wife

return to check the final numbers
gerbil addicted to his wheel

the futures for Tuesday tomorrow
flick my brain on the pillow.

Krewe of Isis

Our house just a block away
the roll of parades—

Saturday morning side streets
packed, saved a spot with trash cans

in front for friends
Bloody Mary's mixed, celery and lime

we've a wagon for the crew
our young boys gear up for throws

stroll to the neutral ground
bands file in to march, we settle

a clear spot, kids wave and yell
an early buzz, we catch loot—

stuffed animals, sunglasses, strands
of beads, rare doubloon

we tire by float forty,
another high school band booms past

my old friend from college dances
with his wife—locals high five tourists

neighbors open doors, offer rest
for the season a slice of king cake.

III.

End of July

Once again the cool blue sky opens
though there's work still to do

this late Friday afternoon lends us freedom.
I stroll with my son down the avenue—

stepping in every puddle, as he excites
at each streetcar passing by

locals eat outdoors at the bistro
toast with globes of Pinot Grigio.

Strangers wave and cross the street
introduce themselves—this is lagniappe

my neighborhood with cathedrals less
than a half mile apart ringing in the evening.

A friend's good advice in May
"enjoy your boy this summer."

Toy Park

At the end of Annunciation Street
a fenced-in acre hugs the river

where my son loves to play—
a place where parents leave

their children's outdoor toys
outgrown, damaged, or weatherworn

the sun strips red tricycles
rain washes blue slides

the toddler lawnmower
still mows the grass

though the horn doesn't beep
there's one trustworthy swing

a bench to rest, let children roam
beneath oaks that clasp like hands

wrestling tropical heat
with their broad shade.

Crib

I did not carve his from wood
rather a little local research

we chose a bluish-grey and white
beauty from Babies R' Us

took my father and I half
a day to construct

a manual thick as a book—

after three years
my son begins the climb out

from this safe harbor, his cell
with stuffed animals where

he often sleeps for ten hours
time to grow into a big boy bed

what should have been a relief
as we put it on the curb for pick up

a burn rose in my throat
our ark sinks slowly into the sea.

Big Boy

Who could not be prouder
in Paw Patrol briefs, graduate

from Spider–Man Pull Ups—
his slow cruise liner away

from diapers…flushing the toilet
a minor reward like putting toys

back in their bin…
now he sleeps

an ark on a wave
a single bed tucked in

with a small zoo of stuffed animals
all in their place

crib just a memory
cast away.

Rhys' Shoe

Midday walk to the post office box
up St. Charles as "ding dings" pass

snack of goldfish from the bag
off to the park—red swing, grey lady

greeting us every day with a flower—
to The Fresh Market, a cool relief

asparagus, fresh lemons, lamb kabobs
roasted almonds, whole milk…

on the way to the car for lunch, check out
a mom carrying her baby

notes he's missing a shoe
back into the store retracing our steps

there on the floor in dairy
it rests like a ruby slipper.

The Littlest Man

Does push-ups at tummy time
To build muscles

Downs a glass of milk
Three times a day with a wide-eyed stare

Needs burping
To avoid hiccups

Prefers to wear a onesy
For his car seat in the rear of the sedan

And catches a nap on the drive
To the grocery

In the produce section, his favorites are baby carrots,
He picks spinach and tiny tomatoes

Likes apples, bananas, pears
Grabs a few blueberries and strawberries

Enjoys seeing his doctor
Getting weighed, cries during his shots

But his favorite things to do
Stroll around the Audubon zoo

He loves the chunky monkey, tigers, elephants,
Flamingos, alligators, and pandas too.

Discipline

My wife claimed *he's an angel*
I knew better—

skip just sixth months
his tantrums, cleverness, gifts

the deal—bargain how
to raise one despite my blood

rising, jaw clench, hand of this father
not clip his wings

too short, as he runs wild across
the green practice field despite

the game, whistle from coach,
another school report

from Miss Clare—throw our hands up
in the air, Christ, he's three

hasn't bitten anyone, yet.

Letting Go

For the past two years
I've picked up my son

from preschool at noon—
today he attends full day

where he naps on his new orange mat
engraved with baseballs matching his lunchbox...

I'm missing him
a knot twists in my chest

miss grabbing
my keys from the bowl

at 11:35, driving down
Jackson deciding whether

to park and walk or take the school carpool...
everyday he's waiting,

sitting on the steps,
a curl in his hair

when he recognizes me
I fill like an empty bottle.

Decadence

*I don't want to belong to any club
that would have me as a member.*
Groucho Marx

I was sponsored and voted on in early spring,
my wife just pregnant for the rum tasting

by the lighthouse of the Southern Yacht Club—
I have a number now, locker, an Olympic

size pool right on the lake—the wait staff
all black, as if we're not in the 21st century

a cordial, awkward place like spending a night
in a guest room or holding a seldom used tool.

They serve fresh redfish and turtle soup,
I get reservations online

high chair and view
of the harbor, kid's menu, crayons

cocktails are generous, stiff, frankly addicting
for this forty-year old grey at the temples

driving my family
the speed limit all the way home.

What's Left

Birthdays, kids, and suicides
The Rolling Stones

Sitting in my office
sun shines bright and slant

marching bands
have stopped

carnival ends as the trash bins
finally empty

the lady across the street with MS has passed
truly a blessing says my elderly neighbor

the bloom on her azaleas
premature

still fall forward with time

zoo's full this morning
children out of school

perhaps I'll ride
to the used bookstore on the streetcar

ease into a wooden bench
and throw open the window

I'll take my toddler along.

Wednesday Morning

Heather has business in New York
asks if I could handle our son

for a few days, *oh sure, no problem*
clothe, bathe, jammies, brush teeth

tasks I'm desperate to accomplish
with ease, there's our puppy Toby

at best house broken, a wild child—
morning rush to pre-school, we're up

with the sunshine, bathroom, breakfast,
outfit and shoes on, bag packed

open the front door Toby escapes
full speed under the gate, I panic

leave our son on the porch begin
the chase my beagle knows the way

while neighbors offer me dog treats
but rather enjoy my sprint, sweat breaks

as he veers in and out of traffic
for a second I lose him, this morning

a dire save, snatch him up in the grass—
my son, a silent saint, waits on our porch

we're all safe, buckle up, a patient drive
little late to class.

Silly Goose

No doubt when your toddler
wises up   goofy behavior

time to take a step back
accept the fact that this

for sure his honest assessment—
I look like a large parrot

hawk maybe raven, more Big Bird
in all his glorious yellow

poking the boy with my beak
as we stroll down the sylvan street.

Big Wheel

My only child pounds pedals
in the empty parking lot

imagine three years ago
life without a monitor

or rear car seat
his mother pregnant

the world's electric, dazzles
each check-up, each day

a new upgrade, nursery,
soft yellow hue

grey crib, and stuffed monkeys
What to Expect When You're Expecting

earmarked on the bedside table
three hearts beating together in bed.

IV.

Pre-Existing Condition

I.

My early teens inked a deal
with the devil

strolling away
from car accidents

falling safe off a cliff in the Rockies,
staying unscarred in schoolyard brawls

not to mention free gifts—
bomber jackets, gold pocket watches

from girls I never asked them for
then to grow, grow into both

boots—after an affair in Northern Ireland,
slipped to Paris and lost

myself praying in empty pews of Saint Chapelle
count of wave over wave in the Seine

re-emerged, bronzed, Rennes,
surfing waves of La Rochelle…

II.

slowed through years, confusion, gin
thoughts of grandeur—narcissism

content like a never-ending
line of credit, deep well, then weight gain—so, so

we began and never ended on a date
when she came down from Madison

a girl now woman eclipsing those teens,
a southern voice, firm constitution

like a baptism, my world was born again.

Dr. D.

The road winds, kisses Lake Michigan
snow slants sideways—my school psychologist

waits on Tuesday and Thursday afternoons
outside parking lot slick with sleet—

punctual, she comes in dark suit or stiff long skirt
to receive me in the waiting room

never takes off her tortoise shell glasses
spreads a wake walking the hall

yet soft spoken, kind in the low light
of her office, window drawn in North Milwaukee.

What we did share across her oriental rug
tugs my despair—not coping

through graduate school, alone
on the top floor of my apartment

we even meet in that cold on a Sunday evening
my final semester in Wisconsin

she holds course like a skiff
barely tacking my way across that icy lake.

Unfit

Things seemed a good fit that morning
sun through windows for my interview

but realized slowly I was not fit for this job
my navy Brooks Brothers felt old and tight,

too snug a fit in her lit office
the executive in a crème blouse

tossed me questions to fumble, pedagogy to family
her crossed, hosed legs physically fit

my resumé littered with gaps of minor success
polished loafers didn't fit her drill

we were lucky—as I rose from the steel chair
I didn't come close to pitching a minor fit

the long stroll out through glass doors
she hoped in my future I'd find a better fit.

Habitat for Humanity

In August heat
I volunteered five days a week

at the central warehouse, not rebuilding
or raising houses rather

stirring used paint cans
moving old porcelain toilets

rewards were pick ups
with Marshall who drove

the delivery truck navigating
neighborhoods, two or three jobs

could take all day when we loitered at lunch—
overstuffed shrimp po-boys

chili-cheese fries, Popeyes fried chicken,
as a mover I saw inside Garden District

homes, contributions stacked in their garages
hauled and unloaded back at the dock, treasures—

oriental rugs, chandeliers, armoires
a few select Marshall left in the back

a wink and nod for his pit stop home
we dusted off the rest and put up for sale.

Beverly

I would stroll hand in hand
down Valence with my grandmother

when dogs were allowed
to poo in the cut grass

she said it's where
they read their newspaper...

Bev drove a deep green Caprice
without a seatbelt, well into

her eighties, her longest drive
across the Causeway

only exceeded when she took us
to Disneyworld after Thanksgiving

pumping gas in Florida, she looked
through the nozzle, we had to flush her eye

she soldiered on feeding us
leftover turkey on the return trip—

she rode a black bicycle over once,
pumped the tires so full

when she left the curb
they popped like gunfire.

Destin

Gulf waves wash green, golden

she angles away
       a despondent shuffle along the strand,

burnt lip of August
       paying no attention much less care

the occupation by teens unleashes
       Nereids with lime daiquiris

baby-oil tans, cans in cuzzis
       Hip-Hop and Buffett…

their end, his calm nap
       disturbed behind designer glasses

the lazy jab of sunlight
       freckles easy

her porcelain skin
       like clear evening stars above the beach

little holds the knots—her chartreuse spaghetti
       straps—the temperature, grate of teeth

a sandal swept out in the surf.

Motorcycle

I still dream about riding one
the same old BMW

I might be at the shop buying her—
riding down sylvan streets...

they're mean streets
young moms driving SUVs on their cell

the obstructed view
hitting the brakes

sends me flying through
an invisible windshield

kissing the pavement
helmeted.

Muriel

A solitary sun he spins
>   woman unknown moves to him

losing orbit, speed intensified
>   like bumper cars collide

how he waits
>   for her to swallow the hook with bait

she's a stretch of tan beach
>   length of legs reach

beneath the hiss of surf an exhale
>   her serape unwraps like a sail

her waist undulates
>   sway of taut stalk of sugarcane

from the local burning field
>   could his fate be sealed—

in his downtown loft sunrise blood red
>   her soft wings spread.

Mata Hari

At her execution
she wears an Amazonian tailored suit,
and new white gloves—

Margaretha Geertruida Zelle
daughter of a Dutch investor

names herself "Eye of the Day"
studies Indonesian and joins
a dance company

famed exotic dancer—
raven haired, olive skinned,
pose of a Hindu
Princess of Javanese birth.

A femme fatale, double agent
she provides her powers of seduction,
undresses the officers—

veils drop until
bearing a jeweled bra, seldom
without, her eagerness to perform
in close to nothing.

Golden Apple

You are free to deceive deceivers.

Ovid, *The Art of Love*

I question the verdict of Paris
a fool's choice of the fairest

for Juno grants power and riches
Minerva glory and renown in war.

I would have weighed the options…
knowing that the golden apple came

from Discord…what a dish Venus
must be, rising from the foam at Cyprus…

to pick the goddess of love and beauty
seems a disaster…for Helen's married

this comes back to bite you poor boy
cause of the Trojan War,

think power, riches, glory, hero
would be surefire temptation

a pretty guy opting for a pretty girl
what about yourself? Your destiny?

Perhaps the end would justify your mean
but not for a war fought over a woman

men of Troy are grateful for your fate
knowing of gorgeous fish in the sea.

Medusa

The locked eye, urge to cry out
hand her a rose,

leading her into a lemon grove

for her beauty barely fades
like a rock in a numbing stream

and if I fix her gaze
any longer

I would harden, crack
my porcelain skin.

The Last Trojan

Came to us a big surprise
his proposal and solitaire accepted.

He pushed and passed forty single—
after years with Penelope, the heiress

Helen, lithe runway model
Sophia, safari photographer,

L. A. now for the modern Aeneas
founding his new nation

in the shadow of the Coliseum
where Traveler rides

under blood orange sunset, waxing moon
with the Pacific's persistent

crashing waves—
calla lilies wash in the surf.

Southern California

Even in May, the Pacific
downright cold, a slip of beach

surrounded by rocks and boulders
       (back on Florence Reginald Denny
        is pulled from his truck)
we're sophomores skipping class

catching a tan, Frisbee in the surf—
       (beaten in daylight—riots, looting
        just blocks from our apartment)
take my weathered Celica

up PCH splurge on Coronas
forget the limes…

just a band of boys from the South
       (knocks on all the doors)
on a long afternoon, discussing
       (no time to pack a bag)

urgent issues—next meal,
       (or call anyone
       we all evacuate)
should we get a dog, who's driving home.

Close Call

Wildfire, riots, return to calm
sunshine persistent

my folks fly from Louisiana
into LAX

take me and a girl for brunch
off Sunset at the Wilshire Hotel—

I recall mimosas, rising from the table
a bit tipsy searching a bathroom

lost in the carpeted lobby
I press a door that locks

behind me, panic on a cement
stairway have to find a dark corner

and relieve myself—
the end justifies the means

at the stair bottom
I empty into a side street

where I jog for the entrance
and return to our table

no one mentions my absence.

Recurrent Dream

No wife, toddler, beagle
in familiar Milwaukee

a cold spring, my ragged apartment on Murray
still paid for, still the stained beige carpet

a highlit view of the city—
dire need to make it to class

in order to graduate—
plunge my old silver motorcycle unhelmeted

through flakes of snow, a Celtic mist
down Oakland to school

nowhere to park
doors illuminated but shut—

there's also practice, for baseball
lucky to make the lineup

for once have this chance, take a cut
that I've been working on, waiting to hit

on deck, my mouth salty with sweat
no crowd in the seats, no pitcher on the mound.

Beau Boudreaux is the author of two collections of poetry, most recent *Rapunzel's Braid* (Five Oaks Press, 2016). His first book of poems is *Running Red, Running Redder* (Cherry Grove Collections, 2012). He currently teaches at Tulane University and lives in New Orleans with his wife and son.

Made in the USA
Columbia, SC
20 September 2019